FUNERALS
&
MEMORIALS

Creating the Perfect Service
to Remember a Loved One

Dayna Reid

Printed in the United States of America
First Printing: May 2015

International Standard Book Number-13: 978-1511604918
 (Softcover)
International Standard Book Number-10: 1511604913
 (Softcover)

Visit the author's website at www.DaynaReid.com

Acknowledgements

I am so grateful to these kind-hearted people for sharing their wealth of experience and the generosity of their time. I would've been lost without their invaluable input on this project. Thank you …

Pastor Harvey Buck
Pastor Wil Mayfield
Pastor Dan Lloyd

Contents

Introduction

"Five hundred twenty five thousand six hundred minutes
How do you measure, measure a year?
In daylights, in sunsets
In midnights, in cups of coffee
In inches, in miles, in laughter, in strife
In five hundred twenty five thousand six hundred minutes
How do you measure, a year in the life?
How about love?
Measure in love
Seasons of love "
*— (From the musical, "**Rent**")*

How do you measure a life? The lyrics to the song, "Seasons of Love" from the Broadway musical "Rent" conclude with, "Measure your life in love."

When a loved one dies, we are compelled to reflect upon the impact they made on our lives and the impression they left on the world. Sometimes this encourages us to take a closer look at our own lives and what is important to us.

While our accomplishments are interesting and provide a glimpse into our personality, the things that really matter at the end of a life are the things we did, which were rooted in love.

When honoring someone who has passed on, we want to highlight their accomplishments and capture the characteristics of their personality, but more importantly, we want to communicate the essence of who they were to the people in their lives.

Last year a friend asked me to officiate my first memorial for a member of their family, whom I'd never met. I'd been officiating weddings for over a decade, but had never had the opportunity to perform a memorial service. I had no clue where to begin.

I started my search online, looking for books and other resources to help with this process. I was unable to find anything that would walk me through the process of what to do, or any variety of wording options for composing the service. So, I reached out to a friend who had performed many memorials—his assistance, combined with my experience creating and officiating weddings, proved to be the perfect compliment to composing a beautiful and meaningful memorial.

After delivering the memorial, the family told me that it was the most beautiful service they'd ever attended, and that the way I'd captured the characteristics of their loved one made them feel like I knew him.

I decided that I'd write a book to share what I'd learned about the delicate process of creating and officiating a memorial, to give others a practical guide to do it themselves.

This book is focused on choosing the best words to accurately and lovingly convey the significance of who a loved one was, to those closest to him or her.

Within these pages you'll find everything you need in order to prepare for and perform a memorial service, including how to interview the family, how to write a eulogy, how to offer support to the grieving, and how to deal with special circumstances regarding the deceased—for example, how to honor someone who was not well-liked in their community.

In addition to the basics of crafting and delivering the service, you'll be guided through the delicate task of gathering information from people who'll likely be distressed, and in the selection of words that prudently and authentically honor their loved one.

Who should read this book?

This book provides anyone asked to participate in a memorial service with everything needed to fulfill that request. Whether you're the person presiding over the entire service or a friend or family member asked to say a few words, you'll find a variety of ideas and information necessary to accomplish your part with sensitivity and grace.

Let's begin the journey of designing a service which genuinely expresses the significance of the impact one person has left on the world, and reflects upon the importance of life itself.

Funerals & Memorials

Who Can Perform the Service

Namely, you.

A funeral or memorial can be conducted by anyone. There are no legal requirements for officiating the service. The primary role of the person performing the service, whether it's a friend, a family member, or a person who didn't know the deceased, is to facilitate the memorial, to make sure that the loved one is honored in the way that the family desires. In this role, also known as the Officiant, you are expected to gather all the information needed about the deceased to create and deliver the service, and to coordinate with the family and the venue regarding any logistics (slide show presentation to be shown during the memorial, music, etc.) pertaining to the service.

The Officiant will also coordinate with friends and family members who wish to participate in the service. This may include reading a poem, saying a few words about their personal relationship with the loved one, or assisting with other aspects of the service such as reading the obituary or passing around a microphone for others to share their memories.

If the memorial will be held in a religious place of worship, the clergy there will usually lead the service. If the memorial will be held in a funeral home, the director of the funeral home can lead the service, or you can invite a clergy member, a friend, a family member or anyone else you choose to officiate. Many memorials are also held in other locations, such as a rented hall or a backyard.

As more people look for alternatives to the traditional, often religious, options for a memorial service, there has been an increase in the number of people offering non-religious Officiant services for funerals and memorials. The people who offer this as a service are typically referred to as an Officiant or Celebrant.

Types of Services

Funerals are for the living . . . to celebrate a life lived.

Funerals and memorials are beneficial to the survivors, not only as a reminder of their own mortality, but also as a means of helping them cope with the loss and begin to adjust to life without their loved one.

The primary difference between the various types of services is whether the service will be formal or informal, and whether or not the deceased's body is present (see the "Disposition of the Body" section in this book for more information about options).

For example, both a funeral and a memorial are services held to honor the deceased person. However, a funeral is typically more formal and the deceased's body is present at the service, while a memorial is typically less formal, and the body is not present. The exception is if the deceased has been cremated and the service is held with the cremated remains present, it is still considered a memorial service.

Memorial
Structure of Service: Informal, Body: Not Present

While there is no specific format for a memorial service, it typically follows a similar format to a funeral service, with the exception of a processional and recessional.

Many people choose this type of service because it honors the deceased in a traditional way, without the formality and expense of a funeral. (See the "Order of Service" section in this book for service options)

Funeral
Structure of Service: Formal, Body: Present

A funeral service typically adheres to a traditional format, with a processional for bringing the casket into the room where the funeral will be conducted, and a recessional for bringing the body to the hearse for transportation to the gravesite and often concludes with a brief graveside service.

After the service, it is customary for everyone to gather in a reception area or at the family home to provide an opportunity for them to convey their thoughts and feelings in a more intimate environment.

Celebration of Life
Structure of Service: Informal, Body: Not Present

A celebration of life service is similar to a memorial, but does not follow any particular format and is not typically held in a church or funeral home, but rather somewhere less formal. For example, an outdoor garden, rented hall, family member's home, or a favorite place of the deceased, and the atmosphere is more like a party.

Wake
Structure of Service: Informal, Body: Present

A wake traditionally takes place in the house of the deceased with the body present. In the United States and Canada the word "wake" has become synonymous with "viewing."

Historically this gathering was for mourners to keep watch or vigil over their dead until they were buried.

Today, wakes are held in funeral homes, as well as pubs, with or without the body present. The wake is less of a service and more of a social "drop-in" where people gather together who cared about the person who has passed on and socialize to reminisce and share the grieving process.

Graveside Service
Structure of Service: Formal, Body: Present

(Sometimes called the "Interment" or "Committal")

The graveside service, also known as the committal, can be the sole service. It's usually briefer than a funeral or memorial service.

This service takes place at the gravesite where the body or the cremated remains will be buried (also known as "interred") and is the final portion of the funeral service.

This service can also be the *only* service. If it is the only memorial performed—doesn't follow a funeral or memorial service—then you will want to include a eulogy in the words spoken at the gravesite. Otherwise, this service will not include a eulogy.

In a cemetery, family and friends will gather near the open grave into which the coffin is partially lowered and the committal is spoken.

Flowers, flower petals, or a handful of sand or soil, can be placed on the coffin as family and friends pay their last respects before the coffin is fully lowered. You can also play music or sing a song, or ring a bell at this time.

Order of Service

Processional (Funeral only)

The coffin is sometimes brought in as part of a processional. The Officiant and the choir (if any) lead the funeral procession and are followed by the pallbearers, two by two. The family follows next, and sometimes, close friends will complete the procession. The family and pallbearers occupy the front rows, with friends on either side.

Opening Words

The words spoken at this time calls together all in attendance to begin the service and welcomes the guests as well as introduces the purpose of the gathering. Prayers or blessings may be included at this time to invoke a higher source (God, Goddess, Great Spirit, the Universe, etc.) to elevate the intent of the memorial.

Obituary Reading

An obituary is a news article that reports the recent death of someone, along with information about the upcoming memorial. Obituaries are commonly painstakingly written by the family and capture aspects of the deceased's life that were important to them. The obituary can be read during the service as a way to honor the effort put forth in composing the obituary as well as to communicate the family's particular perspective. (See the "How to Write an Obituary" section of this book for more information.)

Eulogy

The words spoken at this time are focused on praise of the deceased, the life they lived and the legacy they've left behind. The intention is to provide comfort and/or inspiration to the grieving guests. (See the "How to Write a Eulogy" section of this book for ideas.)

Sermon/Address

This element shares with the guests, the deceased's belief about death and what happens when we die, and is designed to encourage reflection on the significance of life and how we choose to live it.

This may be communicated directly by talking specifically about death and beyond, or it can be conveyed metaphorically through a reading, poem, story or song. (See the "Reading Selections and Sample Wording" section of this book for ideas.)

Final Viewing (funeral only)

This funeral element allows guests the opportunity to say their final goodbye to the deceased by viewing the body of their loved one, for the last time before the body is transported to the gravesite. This can also help provide closure to the grieving.

During the funeral service, the casket will be closed. When the viewing is offered, the casket will be opened and guests will be invited to come forward to pay their last respects.

Closing Words

The words spoken at this time are meant to leave the grieving with a sense of closure, a feeling of comfort and to inspire them to reflect on their own mortality and the importance of making the most of our brief time in this world.

Recessional (funeral only)

A recessional ends the funeral service. The Officiant leads the pallbearers, followed by the coffin (carried or guided by the pallbearers), and then the members of the immediate family. At a memorial service, the Officiant leads the family out through the same door they entered.

It's common practice for one or more of the relatives to stop at the back of the church or outside to briefly thank those who have attended the service.

If the deceased is to be buried following the service, the site of the interment will be announced and a processsional of cars will form to drive to the cemetery.

Personal Memories

Some time during the service could be dedicated to allow guests to share their personal memories of the deceased. A microphone may be passed to each participant or they can take turns standing up to share their thoughts. Because most people don't like to be the first to speak, it's recommended that prior to the service, someone be identified who is willing to go first.

Another possibility for this time of sharing is to have the guests write their thoughts on notecards during the service and then collect the notecards toward the end of the service to be read by the Officiant. The Officiant could read all of the cards, or if it would take too long to read them all, they could choose to select a few and pass along the remaining notes to the family.

Readings

Readings consist of one or more selections (poems, lyrics, stories, etc.) to be read aloud during carefully selected moments throughout the service. The selections are meant to convey a feeling or message that provides a window into the deceased's unique world and may be read by a friend, family member or the Officiant. (See the "Reading Selections and Sample Wording" section for examples.)

Music

Music has the power to set a mood, evoke emotion, and enhance the significance of a moment. The music selected for a memorial service often includes songs or a genre of music that the deceased person enjoyed.

Traditionally, music is played for the Prelude (when the guests are finding seats and waiting for the service to begin), during the Procession, Recession and Postlude (when your guests are exiting). Music may be placed anywhere in the service, for example, after the Eulogy, during a moment of remembrance, or in place of a reading. (See the "Music Ideas" section of this book for possible music selections.)

The Service

Interviewing the Family

"When you lose a parent you lose your past; when you lose a spouse you lose your present; when you lose a child you lose your future." *~(from* ***"A Time to Grieve," Book One)***

Being the Officiant means you are responsible for gathering basic information as well as personal stories from key members of the family. But the most important part of your role is to provide a calm presence—both during the interview as well as during the service—which comforts the family and allows the space and time needed for them to share about their loved one.

Beliefs about Death

It's important to ask about the deceased's beliefs about death: "Tell me about _____'s spiritual beliefs." This will help determine how to talk about the finality of death during the service. For example, if they were atheist, you may want to talk about how their loved one lives on in their heart and memories. If they were Christian, you may want to talk about God and the afterlife. If you don't agree with their beliefs, you will need to put aside your personal beliefs as you work with them to prepare the service, which accurately reflects *their* beliefs. If you strongly disagree with any particular belief that the family wants communicated during the service, you can preface this information with the statement, "The family would like everyone to know that ..." This lets people know that the information is included by specific request of the family, and therefore not necessarily what you believe. You don't have to state that it's not something that you personally believe.

Basic Information Gathering

The "Funeral or Memorial Checklist" section of this book can be used to assist with gathering information vital to the deceased's life. If the person you're interviewing doesn't know the answer to one of your questions, don't stress about it. Simply leave it out or ask if another family member might know the answer.

When interviewing the family, make sure to pronounce names correctly. If you are unsure, ask, and if needed, make a note for yourself of the phonetic pronunciation.

When working with the family, refer to the deceased by name. Also, ask if there is a nickname they would like you to use and use it, both during the interview process and during the service. Mentioning their loved one by name helps make the process feel personal to the family.

While gathering basic information, make a special note of the deceased's birthday and wedding anniversary (if applicable). Follow up with a note or card on the next birthday and/or anniversary (See the "After the Service – Following Up" section of this book for more information).

Depending on the circumstances surrounding the death, the family may or may not want you to include specifics in the service. You can ask them how their loved one died; "How did ___ die?" Then, follow up by asking, "Do you want me to mention how ___ died in the memorial service?" Allow the family to dictate what information is shared during the service.

In addition to the wishes of the family for the memorial service, sometimes the deceased, before they died, shared desires of their own. If appropriate (obviously you would not ask this about a child), you can ask the family "Did ____ have any specific wishes for their memorial service that you are aware of?"

The Obituary

If it exists, an obituary can be a good resource for finding basic information and to complete many items on your checklist. Sometimes the family may request that you read the obituary word for word during the service. While it does communicate the vital statistics, incorporating these same facts into an address may seem more natural and personal.

Thoughts, Sentiments, and Stories

General information is not enough. To truly tell the story of the loved one, you will need to draw-out more personal information from key members of the family. This can be done through an interview process that will include asking the right questions and actively listening to the answers. Think about what the guests will want to know about the deceased to give them a clear picture of the loved one's life. For example, what does the family think the deceased would have wanted to be remembered for most?

The Officiant is responsible for gathering and communicating the finer details of the deceased's life.

The Interview Process

Determine the right person or people to interview. The most obvious choice is not always the best choice. Use the family's recommendations combined with your own judgment to determine the right person or people to approach for the best information. This may not be limited to strictly family members, but perhaps could include a good friend or coworker. Always defer to the family's wishes, however, as their opinion is the most important.

If possible, select a meeting place that is private or semi-private. You will want the people being interviewed to be in a comfortable setting where they feel free to express their emotions and where they don't feel rushed.

Keep in mind that the family member you are interviewing may not be in a good place emotionally to volunteer information or effectively articulate stories or nuances about their loved one's life. While some people may be visibly distraught, others may seem less emotional than you expect. Remember that even if the family representative seems to be in "business mode," that does not mean they don't care. Either way, it's your job to draw out the needed information in a calming, soothing manner.

For instance, "Uncle Bob really loved football." Some follow-up questions you might ask are: Did Bob ever play football himself? What was his favorite team? Are there any stories you can tell me about a time when he did something extraordinary to not miss a game?

The key to being a good interviewer is first and foremost being a good listener. Don't listen for just the words, but notice the body language and listen to the emotions behind the words as well. Use your observations to truly tell a story about their loved one.

Handling Special Circumstances

In each of these special circumstances, it is important to acknowledge the negative while focusing on the positive. For example, in the case of a sudden death, by briefly mentioning the tragic nature of the circumstances, it helps the loved ones come to terms with what has happened. But it is then vital to move on to the more positive focus of the deceased's legacy and how they will "live on" in the hearts and minds of their loved ones.

Or in the case of a deceased person who was disliked by many, the emphasis could be on moments in their life that demonstrate their strengths, while recognizing their difficult personality (possibly by using humor).

The following are four examples of special circumstances with some suggested wording for introducing the eulogy.

Sudden/Tragic Death

Car crash. Overdose. Heart Attack. Murder. What do you say when there are no words? How do you provide comfort when there is none? How do you make sense of a senseless tragedy?

When the person's death is unexpected, the initial shock and disbelief is often greater and lasts longer than when we have some warning. The suddenness of the loss is overwhelming, doesn't make sense and is hard to believe.

When creating the eulogy, you will want to acknowledge and talk about this state of "shock" that most people will be experiencing—to reassure them that they're not alone in what they're feeling.

Here are sample introductions to the eulogy for someone who has died suddenly and/or tragically.

Wording Choice #1

As we gather here today, still in shock from the (sudden/tragic) death of (name), we're numb, scared and angered at the unfairness and senselessness that took (him/her) from us. We seek to make sense of this, to understand the reason why this happened. Unfortunately, there are no easy answers, and as difficult and painful as it is, we must acknowledge our loss, the loss to all of us that (his/her) passing brings, and acknowledge the great importance of (name)'s life.

And though we must bravely face this sad time, we owe it to (name), and to ourselves, to look at the bigger picture of (his/her) life.

Let's take a closer look at (name)'s life and celebrate what (his/her) life has meant to us and the legacy (he/she) has left the world.

Wording Choice #2

Those of us gathered here today have been touched by violence and hatred. Our hearts ache as we experience the pain of this tragic loss. Our thoughts and prayers are for (name), whose life has been cut short, and for those of us who will forever be changed by the intrusion of violence.

Although we're familiar with the impact violence has on our world, this tragedy invades places where we should feel safe and we may find ourselves sad, afraid, and angry.

Today, may we be comforted and somehow find meaning in this senseless loss as we're reminded of the fragility of life.

As we honor the life of (name), this is our prayer:
May we find hope in the face of life's horrors.
May we have the courage to hold true to our beliefs and
our values, even when they are most severely tested.
And may we draw upon the invisible reservoir of love,
in us and among us, to heal a wounded world and cre-
ate peace.

Suicidal Death

When someone takes their own life, the main questions on the minds of the people close to them are, "Why?" and "What could I have done to prevent it?"

When creating the eulogy, you will want to acknowledge and talk about these questions that most people will be asking themselves—to reassure them that they're not alone in what they're feeling and that there is nothing they could've done to prevent their loved one's death.

Because this type of death was *chosen*, the approach you take to the eulogy is particularly delicate. Some family members may be heartbroken over the suffering that caused their loved one to make this decision. Others may be angry at their loved one for choosing to leave them with overwhelming responsibilities that should've been shared (such as the raising of the deceased's children).

Take time to understand the feelings of the family about their loved one's decision, and honor these feelings in the eulogy, by speaking words that are not completely contrary to how another family member feels. For example, if the deceased's widow is furious at his or her loved one for leaving him or her to raise their children alone, you may not want to spend too much time empathizing with the suffering of the deceased that lead to this decision.

Here are sample introductions to the eulogy for someone who has committed suicide.

Wording Choice #1

We're here today with a variety of emotions as deep and complex as the (man/woman) we are remembering. There is love—and the agonizing pain of separation. There is anger—and the futile search to understand why (name) kept (his/her) pain to (himself/herself). Why didn't (he/she) reach out and ask for help? Some of you may ask what you could've done to prevent it.

Let's remember that no single act of desperation can define a life. (Name)'s life also had its moments of delight and happiness, caring and friendship, sharing and love. Death by choice is not a denial of life; it's the cry of agony for more life. It grows from a deep personal alienation or profound suffering, and is carried out alone, after a struggle within the self. When a death such as this cuts across life in its fullness, we feel incomplete.

We know that (name) leaves much unfinished, unfulfilled, unsaid. The sadness for the loss of life is compounded by the sadness for the loss of possibilities not realized. But we must remember that the life (name) did live, made an impact on our lives, and did not go unnoticed. We will now take this time to reflect on (name)'s life and celebrate the person that (he/she) was, and the ways (he/she) will live on in our hearts.

Wording Choice #2

On (date of death), (name) completed a decision. Where there is pain and confusion, despair and doubt, we long for the end to suffering. For some, like (name), life seems to no longer offer any choice but one. Life can inflict pain that we cannot find the inner resources to heal. The inner pain for (name) was too great and (he/she) chose to end the suffering for (himself/herself). However, the suffering does not end for (his/her) loved ones. Friends and family are left with feelings of shock, betrayal, anger and sadness. Left to ask, "Why didn't I know? What could I have done to prevent it?" But there is nothing we could've done and in time, these feelings will evolve into compassion and forgiveness for (name) and in time, we will come to accept that this was out of our control.

We now honor (name)'s memory and support one another in grieving a death that is the hardest death to grieve: death that is chosen. Let's look at the ways (name) has touched our lives and how (he/she) will live on in our hearts.

Infant or Child Death

The loss of a child is the most traumatizing of all—the most difficult to accept. A Seattle area clergy member, Pastor Harvey Buck, shared this example of the shock that the family experiences, in an account of a funeral he did for an infant. He said that he saw the mother of the child a year after the memorial and she said, "Thanks for doing the memorial, I heard it was really great." She had attended the memorial, but she wasn't really *there*.

Not only do we grieve the loss of their life, but we are also tormented by our unrealized dreams for their future. Similar to other sudden deaths, there are no words to help us make sense of the senseless.

When creating the eulogy, you will want to acknowledge and talk about not only the briefness of the life lived, but also the loss of hopes and dreams for their future.

Here is a sample introduction to the eulogy for an infant or a child who has passed on.

Grief for the loss of a child is hardest to bear. When a child dies, we mourn not only the life that was, but also the life that might have been.

Victor Frankl once said, "We cannot judge a biography by its length, by the number of pages in it; we must judge by the richness of the contents. Sometimes the unfinished are among the most beautiful symphonies."

Let's now take a look at the brief and precious life of (name) and how (he/she) touched our lives and how (he/she) will live on in our hearts.

Unpopular Personality of the Deceased

It can be challenging to find something positive to say about someone who was unpopular or disliked by their family and/or their community. For example, if the deceased had a difficult personality and tended to show disdain for everyone in their life, the family may have a tough time recalling positive memories that could be used in the eulogy. Or if the deceased was a well-known criminal, such as a convicted pedophile or serial killer, there may not be anything positive that the family wants to offer.

One question you can ask the family is, "What one or two things can you say about ___ that are true, but charitable?" The family may have to go far back in history to dig up something positive, but there is usually something you can say, even if it's something as simple as telling a story about a time in their childhood when the person behaved considerately. For example, "When Joe was young, his dog

Benji was his best friend and he would rush home from school to be with him and would take him everywhere he went."

If the family is unable to come up with anything specific that is positive, you can use euphemisms to focus on his/her challenging nature and the end of the struggle. For example, "It was a tough road that we shared with ____. There were many stones and obstacles along the way. But (his/her) soul has finally found peace." Or, you can be vague while addressing the bad things that they did by using a phrase like, "(his/her) strength of character morphed into weakness" without mentioning the specific deeds.

The key is to focus on the positive and also acknowledge the negative without being specific or dwelling there. It's important to be authentic about the negative aspects of the deceased's life in order for people to move on, but it's not necessary to talk about the details.

Funeral or Memorial Checklist

The following is a checklist of possible information to gather for planning the service:

❑ Type of service: Funeral, Memorial, Celebration of Life, etc.

❑ Date of birth, date of death.

❑ Location of birth and childhood.

❑ Full birth name. Full married name.

❑ Parents' names.

❑ Siblings' names.

❑ Spouses' names.

❑ Children and Grandchildren's names.

❑ Personality traits. (Always kind, mostly grouchy, etc.)

❑ Education.

❑ Vocation.

❑ Significant life events.

❑ Significant events surrounding the death.

❑ Prayers to include. (Are there any favorites of the deceased?)

❑ Scriptures to include. (Are there any favorites of the deceased?)

❑ Readings to include. (Are there any favorites of the deceased?)

❑ Music to include. (Are there any favorites of the deceased?)

  -Format of music. (Recorded, live, sung, etc.)

  -Timing of music. (Opening, closing, etc.)

❑ Testimonials of others to include. (Spoken by officiant, open mic, note cards, etc.)

How to Write a Eulogy

The word *eulogy* means, "to bless." It comes from the Greek word "eulogia" which means, "praise," "blessing" or "something blessed." So, the eulogy is an opportunity to "praise" and "give thanks" for the life of the loved one that has passed on.

A eulogy conveys the deceased's personality traits and memorable times that were shared with friends and family, as well as giving a condensed history of their life, which includes highlights of important accomplishments. A eulogy can also include the deceased's favorite poems, readings, scripture, quotes, or something that was written by them. The content and selections should reflect the character and lifestyle of the deceased, and be written in an informal, conversational tone.

Questions to help you begin the process:

- Is there a humorous or touching story that represents the essence of _____?
- What did people love and admire about _____?
- What will people miss most about him or her?
- Now that _____ is gone, what is missing in the world?
- If _____ could say something at the service, what would they say?

Information to include in the eulogy:

- If you knew the deceased personally, you could include a short introduction about yourself and your relationship to them.
- A brief biography of the deceased person.
- Information about his or her career.

- Comments about his or her family, friends and pets.
- Summary of achievements.
- Favorite songs or poems.
- Information about hobbies or interests.
- Personal stories of friends and family.

Tips

- Interview family and friends, and use direct quotes in the eulogy where possible to personally connect with those who've provided their heartfelt memories.
- Be honest and focus on the person's positive qualities. If the deceased had some significantly negative qualities, briefly acknowledge them, but don't dwell on them (See the "Handling Special Circumstances" section of this book for more information).
- Humor is acceptable if it fits the personality of the deceased and the family.
- Keep in mind that some of the simplest memories can be deeply touching. For example, "We'll miss his smile," or "We'll never forget the way she crinkled her nose when she laughed."
- Give a copy of the draft to the family for final approval.

Here is an excerpt from of an actual eulogy written for a family of a man who died unexpectedly of lung cancer.

Charles Worth Gossett, was born in Charlotte, North Carolina, on November 20, 1945. And so began the life of the man that the people gathered here today were proud, honored and privileged to call their father ... their grandfather ... their son ... their brother and their friend.

31

Worth had two children, Randy and Alison. Two brothers, Clay and Benjy. And a sister, Rose, who passed away when she was only 40.

He also had a brother, Jim and a sister, Jamie, from his father's second marriage, whom he had never met until a year and a half before his death, when he began his quest to learn everything he could about his father. Upon meeting his new extended family, which included his father's second wife, Patti, and her children and grandchildren, he developed a close relationship with them in a very short time.

Patti and Worth bonded quickly, as Patti helped Worth search for military records and historical information about his father.

They were all crazy about each other and affectionately referred to the families as the "West Coast and East Coast Gossett's." In the words of his sister, Jamie, "God gave us a glimpse of time with him and we made the most of it. I believe my life is better for knowing him."

He was an amazing, warm-hearted man who desired to share his life with everyone, and within the span of his cut-too-short life, managed to fulfill all of his childhood dreams. At age 12, he was awarded "The Knight of the Rose." At age 19, he joined the Army and served 4 years. He then took a couple of years off to be a beach bum. He rejoined the Army in 1977 and retired in 1988. He was a pilot who flew Cobras and Mohawks. He was a non-commissioned officer—"Chief Warrant Officer 4"—and was one of only 15 non-commissioned officers in the Army to be given the honor of becoming a commissioned officer. He served in Vietnam and was a true war hero. He earned a Bronze Star, Silver Star, The Meritorious Service Medal, the Air Medal, the Distinguished Flying Cross, the Army Commendation Medal, a couple of Purple Hearts as well as many other medals. When he retired from the Army, he joined the police force and became a detective. When he retired from the police force, he became a park ranger and part of his job was rounding up and killing the feral hogs. They were mean and dangerous, and he was nearly taken down by them several times. He used to joke and call himself a "hog killer." After that, he became a writer for "The Aviator" magazine.

His nephew, Boog, recently shared this about Worth: "Worth was a hero, not in his own eyes, but in the eyes of the people who loved him. He led a very extreme life and was a macho man. In a few months of Skyping in the early afternoon and long phone calls, I learned so much about him that even his closest friends may not have known. I truly enjoyed and was impressed with him as a whole. He helped open me up to new interests and even increased some of them!"

At the age of 66, after only 3 short months of illness, Worth's body succumbed to lung cancer, and on July 31, 2012, he fell asleep in the arms of God.

Officiating the Service

The duration of your portion of the service should be limited to approximately twenty minutes. This provides adequate time to honor the deceased without being too lengthy, and also leaves time for other aspects of the service (i.e. greetings, refreshments, etc.) You have two main goals as the Officiant: one is to create and deliver a eulogy, which appreciates the family's wishes for honoring their loved one; and the other is to be "present" and "available" to the family before, during and after the service.

Arrival

When you arrive at the memorial service location, connect with the appointed family member/s to coordinate and offer help with any last minute details. Arrive early to allow enough time to be of assistance if needed, as well as to provide a sense of reassurance to the family, that you are the anchor in their sea of distress and confusion.

An Officiant in the Seattle area, Pastor Dan Lloyd, eases the family's anxiety with these words of advice, he tells them: "Your only job at the memorial service is to *show up and let people love you.*"

No Magic Words, Just Be Present

During the service, "Be *present*," says, Seattle area chaplain, Pastor Wil Mayfield. "Sometimes we say too much. When people are dealing with extreme loss, *less* is definitely more; it's better to simply be available than to try to find words to comfort the inconsolable."

No words can effectively minimize the pain they are feeling, so, resist the urge to fill the silence with words. Your primary role is to simply "be there," to be a source of calm assurance; someone they can lean on when needed. Tell them, "I'll be right over here if you need anything."

The following, written by Molly Fumia in "Safe Passage," beautifully expresses the act of being present:

"I'll cry with you', she whispered 'until we run out of tears. Even if it's forever. We'll do it together.'

There it was ... a simple promise of connection. The loving alliance of grief and hope that blesses both our breaking apart and our coming together again."

Some words or phrases may be extremely painful for the grieving to hear. Clichés diminish the loss by providing simple answers to an extremely difficult reality. A comment like: "You still have so much to be thankful for" is not helpful and can even make their grieving more difficult. (See the "Understanding Grief" section of this book for more information.)

There is no need to be somber—just be *genuine*, composed, and available. If you make a mistake during the service, don't try to hide it, simply acknowledge your error and move on—own your mistakes.

Payment for Officiant Services

The payment given to an Officiant for providing memorial services is referred to as an *honorarium; a payment given for a professional service provided for free.*

Most clergy will conduct a funeral for no charge, but it is customary to give them an honorarium. The amount offered is up to the family, based on what they can afford. Often, the funeral home they are working with will pay this honorarium to you, on their behalf. Whenever possible, it is best to work with a funeral home to determine amount and form of payment and to avoid talking about money with the family.

Music Ideas

Music can be much more powerful and evocative than spoken word. The lyrics, the melody, and the way the song is arranged can further enhance the intended atmosphere. For example, the lyrics to the song, "Amazing Grace," could be included on the memorial program given to the attendees, and the song could be sung acapella to close the service, which may be more powerful than playing a pre-recorded version of the song.

The placement of the music within the service can shift the mood. For example, you may want to choose opening music with a reflective quality and then close with something more celebratory to end the memorial on a lighter note.

Here are some ideas for memorial music:

Reflective Songs

- Amazing Grace - sung acapella or Michael Crawford
- Angel - Sarah McLachlan
- Ave Maria
- Because You Loved Me - Celine Dion
- Bridge Over Troubled Waters - Simon and Garfunkel
- Bright Eyes - Art Garfunkel
- Dance With My Father - Luther Vandross
- Fly - Celine Dion
- Imagine - John Lennon
- Jealous of the Angels - Jenn Bostic
- Longer - Dan Fogelberg
- May It Be - Enya

- My Heart Will Go On - Celine Dion
- Nearer my God to Thee (Hymn)
- One Sweet Day - Mariah Cary
- The Prayer - Celine Dion
- Stairway to Heaven - Led Zeppelin
- Taps - (Instrumental: Military)
- Tears in Heaven - Eric Clapton
- The Upper Room (Hymn)
- To Where You Are - Josh Groban
- Unforgettable - Nat King Cole
- When You're Gone - Avril Lavigne
- Wind Beneath My Wings - Bette Midler
- You Are So Beautiful to Me - Joe Cocker
- You Raise Me Up (Hymn) - Westlife

Celebratory Songs

- Always Look on the Bright Side of Life - Monty Python
- Circle of Life - Elton John
- Don't You Forget About Me - Simple Minds
- Goin up Yonder (Hymn)
- I'll Be Missing You - Puff Daddy
- In My Life - The Beatles
- My Way - Frank Sinatra
- Over The Rainbow - Eva Cassidy
- Season of Love (from the play, "Rent")
- Seasons in the Sun - Terry Jacks or Westlife
- Spirit in the Sky - Norman Greenbaum
- We'll Meet Again - Vera Lynn or Johnny Cash
- What a Wonderful World - Louis Armstrong
- You'll Never Walk Alone - Gerry and the Peacemakers

Additional Service Ideas

Here are some ideas to further personalize the memorial service.

Food and Beverages

Depending on the location of the service, light refreshments, a buffet or a catered meal may be served. Guests may also be invited to gather at someone's home or a nearby restaurant after the service.

Memorial Program

A simple brochure or program outlining the service may be given to all who attend as a keepsake of the event. The program often includes: the loved one's date of birth, date of death, a picture, and a special poem, scripture, or other written words meaningful to the family.

Memory Table

Photos and personal items of the deceased may be displayed on a table. For example, if he or she was a member of the military, you could display their uniform, an American flag, medals or commendations, military pictures, discharge papers, letters, etc.

Video Slideshow

A video slideshow highlighting the deceased's life may be shown at a designated time during the service or in the background as people are gathering for the service. If the slideshow is to be played in the background, it's recommended to pause it during the speaking portion of the service to prevent distracting the guests from being able to give their full attention to the speaker.

Memorial Notecards

On card stock or index cards, guests can write a note to the family or a favorite memory of the deceased. The cards are then placed in a special container and given to the family.

Keepsakes

Memorial keepsakes are gifts distributed at the service that help guests remember their loved one after the service is over. These keepsakes can include memorial bookmarks, prayer cards, candles, charms, etc. For example, personalized cards containing embedded flower seeds can be given to guests to plant. The blooming flowers will serve as a reminder of their loved one long after the memorial.

Balloon Release

At the end of the service, guests can launch biodegradable (latex) balloons into the sky simultaneously, symbolizing letting go of the loved one and letting the grieving process begin. Before releasing the balloon, one can give it a kiss, say a prayer, or write a personal message on it. When released into the air, each person will have a different experience as they let go of their balloon. This activity is most commonly included for the memorial of a child.

Butterfly Release

Many believe that butterflies symbolize spirit, representing freedom, beauty, and new life as they take flight. There are several companies that will deliver live butterflies to your memorial location on the day of your service. At the end of the service, some words can be spoken to honor the loved one as guests release the butterflies simultaneously.

Dove Release

The releasing of white doves symbolizes the beginning of the grieving process and "letting go." There are several companies that will deliver the white birds to your memorial service location. When they are released at the end of the service, they will soar into the sky, usually circling several times in a group before returning to their home.

Guestbook

A guestbook can be made available for guests to sign and leave words of support and encouragement for the family.

Military

If the deceased served in the military and will not be honored with a military funeral, here are a couple of things that are commonly part of a military funeral that could be incorporated into the memorial.

Present a Pre-folded American Flag

Present a pre-folded American flag to the mother or spouse during the service. These can be purchased online.

Play the Song "Taps"

Play the song "Taps" during the service and conclude with a military salute, or play the song with the lowering of the casket. The lyrics to this song could also be read aloud, before or after the song is played.

Taps (lyrics)
(This is one version; there are no official lyrics)

Day is done, Gone the sun,

From the lakes, From the hills, From the sky,
All is well, Safely rest, God is nigh.

Go to sleep, Peaceful sleep,
May the soldier, Or sailor, God keep,
On the land, Or the deep, Safe in sleep.

Love, good night. Must thou go?
When the day And the night Need thee so?
All is well. Speedeth all, To their rest.

Fades the light, And afar,
Goeth day, and the stars Shineth bright,
Fare thee well, Day has gone, Night is on.

Fading light Dims the sight,
And a star Gems the sky, Gleaming bright
From afar, Drawing nigh, Falls the night.

Thanks and praise, For our days,
Neath the sun, Neath the stars, Neath the sky.
As we go, This we know, God is nigh.

Reading Selections and Sample Wording

Opening Words, Prayers and Blessings

The Dash

You'll notice on the front of your program, below (*name*)'s name are the dates when (he/she) was born and when (he/she) passed away. (*date*) "dash" (*date*). We all have a date when we entered this world. We'll all have a date when we'll leave this world. The "dash" is how we lived our life. We don't get to pick our date of birth, or our date of death, but we do get to choose how we spend the time in-between.

(_Name_)'s "dash" was filled with love, with life, and with bringing joy to many during (his/her) time on earth.

As a (father/mother), (grandfather/grandmother), (brother/sister), (uncle/aunt) and dear friend to many, (he/she) will be remembered by each of us as someone who touched our lives.

Today is a time of remembrance and celebration of (name)'s life, and all that (he/she) taught us about living.

The Bible says, "To be absent from the body is to be present with the Lord." From the moment (_name_) breathed (his/her) last breath here on Earth, (he/she) was instantly at home in the presence of God and (his/her) family, surrounded by peace and joy!

We meet here today to honor and pay tribute to the life of (_name_), and to express our love and admiration for (him/her).

Welcome, my name is (_name_), and it's a great privilege and honor for me to be here today to officiate at the (funeral/memorial) of such a well liked and respected (man/woman).

In the words of James T. Kirk:

"We are assembled here today to pay final respects to our honored dead. And yet it should be noted, in the midst of our sorrow, this death takes place in the shadow of new life, the sunrise of a new world; a world that our beloved comrade gave his life to protect and nourish. He did not feel this sacrifice a vain or empty one, and we will not debate his profound wisdom at these proceedings. Of my friend, I can only say this: Of all the souls I have encountered in my travels, his was the most … human."

~*James T. Kirk* *(Star Trek II: The Wrath of Khan)*

I know that today is a sad day, but I hope at the end of this service for (*name*) that you will feel glad that you took the opportunity to grieve in the presence of others who have known and loved (him/her).

The death of someone we dearly love, someone we've shared the best part of our lives with, can sometimes seem like too much to bear, the pain of grief and the sense of loss is immense and often overwhelming. (*Name*) had a good and varied life. In the short time we have here today, we can barely scratch the surface, but I hope when you leave here, you will do so with a sense of having shared in something special, for a very special and unique (man/woman).

We have come together from different places, and we're all at different stages on our journey through life. Our paths are varied and we look at life in different ways. But there is one thing we all have in common, at one point or another, and to some degree or other, our lives have been touched by the life of (*name*).

We are here this (morning/afternoon) in order to pay our last respects and bid a sad but fond farewell to (*name*). We're also here so that, in our own way, we can celebrate, honor and pay tribute to (his/her) life, and in doing so, we express our sincere love and admiration for (him/her).

And so today we've put aside our usual daily activities for a while, and gathered here to give expression to the thoughts and feelings that occupy us at this time of loss, and because, in one way or another, (*name*)'s death affects us all.

The separateness, the uniqueness of each human life is the basis of grief in bereavement. Look through the whole world and there is no one like (*name*). (He/She) still lives on in your memories, and though no longer a visible part of our lives, (he/she) will always remain a member of your family and of your circle, through the influence (he/she) has had on you and the special part (he/she) played in your lives.

The catastrophe of death cannot be altered, but it can be transformed by love. We can share our grief, and I hope you will not feel ashamed or embarrassed to weep openly if this helps.

When someone is taken from us, as (*name*) was, in the prime of their life, understandably we're not as comfortable with phrases that point towards celebrating their life.

Immense anger, deep hurt, inconsolable grief, rage, and disbelief, are just a few of the feelings that are associated with thoughts of (_name_). But hidden in all the pain and sorrow that we feel, there is undeniably something to celebrate. We can celebrate the fact that we have known (_name_), and though (he/she) is no longer with us we can celebrate that we were privileged and honored to have known (him/her).

We gather together today to remember the life of (_name_). We gather to comfort each other in our grief and to honor the life (he/she) led. A life that was full of hope, happiness, laughter, and love ... through good times as well as in bad. This is the way we will always remember (_name_) ... that (he/she) lived (his/her) life as an example to each and every person (he/she) met.

Closing Words, Prayers and Blessings

Father in Heaven,

   We thank you because you made us in your own image and gave us gifts in mind, body and spirit. We thank you now for (_name_) and what (he/she) meant to each of us—the gift that (he/she) was to each of our lives. As we honor (his/her) memory, make us more aware that you are the one from whom comes every perfect gift.

   Amen.

Prayer of St. Francis of Assisi

Lord, make me an instrument of thy peace.
Where there is hatred, let me sow love;
Where there is injury, pardon;
Where there is doubt, faith;
Where there is despair, hope;
Where there is darkness, light;
Where there is sadness, joy.

O divine Master, grant that I may not so much seek
To be consoled as to console,
To be understood as to understand,
To be loved as to love;
For it is in giving that we receive;
It is in pardoning that we are pardoned;
It is in dying to self that we are born to eternal life.

When you leave here in a short while, I hope; that like me, you will leave with a feeling of having shared in something special, for a very special (man/woman).

Let's remind ourselves that the dead reside not in the grave or an urn, but in the hearts and minds of the living.

Hold on to (*name*) in your thoughts, there is no need to part from (him/her) too hastily. Talk about (him/her) often, repeat the words and sayings (he/she) used, and the jokes (he/she) made, and enjoy your memories of (him/her); just as we have here today.

We thank you for the days of life that you gave to (*name*).

May (*name*)'s memory live long among us and be a source of strength for us.

In the midst of the loss we feel as we experience the death of one we love, keep us in touch also with the memories, which can sustain us.

May we find the courage to face the changes which life presents to us as we go on from here. Give to those who most deeply feel this loss the comfort of your presence, and enable each of us to minister to those who mourn.

Amen.

There is no answer to death but to live and to live vigorously and beautifully. We give respect and dignity to the one we mourn, only when we respect and dignify life, and when we live life to the fullest. The best of all answers to death is the continuing affirmation of life. Now, for us, the living, may the love of friends, the joy of memories, and our hopes for the future give us strength and peace that we may go forward together.

~Gail Mccabe

In sadness for (*name*)'s death, but with appreciation for (his/her) life, we remember (*name*) and (his/her) capacity for joy and love. Finally, as we leave to continue our own voyage of discovery in the world, let's listen to the words of this (prayer/poem/song).

~Gail Mccabe

There are miles behind you,
And many more ahead.
As you journey on toward wholeness,
May all that is good and true guide your way.
May the joy of love lighten every step,
And the miracle that is life be ever in your sight.
Live boldly and fully.
True to yourself and all that you hold dear.
Go in peace.
Go in truth.
Go in love.

~Rev. Andy Pakula

Deep within you,
There is a place of peace.

A place of wisdom,
A place of love.
May this sacred center be your guide.
May it be your strength for the journey.
May it fill you with hope when all seems hopeless.
And may it lead you to know the sacredness in all.

~Rev. Andy Pakula

As we prepare to part, let us each be ready to look again.
To look beneath the surface of our lives,
Beneath the rough exteriors we encounter.
For the beauty and love within,
And may this change us.

~Rev. Andy Pakula

Spirit of life and source of love,
Let us feel and know in our bones the wild generosity of existence.
Let us sense in each nurturing taste of the earth's fruits, the life that dances among stars.
Let us find more moments of awakening—where we may more fully appreciate the extravagant beauty of the earth and its living things.
And when we suffer—fear or grief or pain our only companion. Let these wonders be a balm to our troubled souls,
And reawaken us to joy.

~Rev. Andy Pakula

We hold now, in our hearts and minds, the sorrows and disappointments that have recently touched us.

Despite its sorrows, the world is overflowing with beauty and goodness.

We swell with gratitude and feel our own burdens lightened and faith restored as we bring to mind the joys that have preceded this moment in time.

Spirit of life—source of love and light—hold us in all the delights and terrors of this life.

May we have the strength to bear the hardships we face and the wisdom to mine their depths to support our growth toward wholeness.

May we have the generosity to share our joys—and the grace to celebrate the joys of others.

And may we have the vision to recognize the miracle; in every flower petal and tree, every creeping and crawling thing, and in the eyes of each of our fellow travelers.

~Rev. Andy Pakula

We can't know why some things happen ... but we can know that love and beautiful memories outlast the pain of grief. And we can know that there's a place inside the heart where love lives always ... and where nothing beautiful can ever be forgotten.

~Author Unknown

The light of a distant star continues to reach the earth long after the star itself is gone. In the same way, the light and love (*name*) gave will continue to shine in many hearts.

Love never dies; it lives on in your heart forever. Listen carefully, (*name*) will speak to your heart.

Within our hearts and in our memories, those we love remain with us always.

Grief diminishes as memories nourish the heart.

Someone who has truly touched us will always be close through the joy of memories and the beauty of love.

Even as the sun goes down to end the light of day, it's rising on a new horizon somewhere far away.

There's peace in the promise that life is everlasting.

Deep in the heart, steadfast and devout, there burns the light of love that grief cannot put out.

General Readings

Season of Love *(lyrics from the musical, "Rent")*

Five hundred twenty five thousand six hundred minutes
How do you measure, measure a year?
In daylights, in sunsets
In midnights, in cups of coffee
In inches, in miles, in laughter, in strife
In five hundred twenty five thousand six hundred minutes
How do you measure, a year in the life?
How about love?
Measure in love
Seasons of love (love)
Five hundred twenty five thousand six hundred minutes
Five hundred twenty five thousand journeys to plan
How do you measure the life of a woman or a man?
In truths that she learned
Or in times that he cried
In bridges he burned or the way that she died
It's time now, to sing out
Though the story never ends
Let's celebrate
Remember a year in the life of friends
Remember the love
(Oh, you got to, you got to remember the love)
Remember the love
(You know that love is a gift from up above)
Remember the love

(Share love, give love, spread love)
Measure in love
(Measure, measure your life in love)

Biography

One day my life will end; and lest
Some whim should prompt you to review it,
Let her who knows the subject best
Tell you the shortest way to do it:
Then say, 'Here lies one doubly blest.'
Say, 'She was happy.' Say, 'She knew it.'

~Jan Struther

Where the Sidewalk Ends

There is a place where the sidewalk ends
And before the street begins
And there the grass grows soft and white.
And there the sun burns crimson bright,
And there the moon-bird rests from his flight
To cool in the peppermint wind.
Let us leave this place where the smoke blows black
And the dark street winds and bends.
Past the pits where the asphalt flowers grow
We shall walk with a walk that is measured and slow,
And watch where the chalk white arrows go,
To the place where the sidewalk ends.
Yes, we'll walk with a walk that is measured and slow,
And we'll go where the chalk white arrows go,

For the children, they mark, and the children, they know
The place where the sidewalk ends.

~*Shel Silverstein (from "Where the Sidewalk Ends")*

Ascension

And if I go,
while you're still here ...
Know that I live on, vibrating to a different measure—
behind a thin veil you cannot see through.
You will not see me,
so you must have faith.
I wait for the time when we can soar together again—
both aware of each other.
Until then, live your life to its fullest.
And when you need me,
Just whisper my name in your heart ... I will be there.

~*Colleen Corah Hitchcock*

From "The Prophet"

Your fear of death is but the trembling
of the shepherd when he stands before the king
whose hand is to be laid upon him in honor.
Is the shepherd not joyful beneath his trembling,
that he shall wear the mark of the king?
Yet is he not more mindful of his trembling?
For what is it to die but to stand naked
in the wind and to melt in the sun?
And what is it to cease breathing,
but to free the breath from its restless tides,
that it may rise and expand and seek God unencumbered?

Only when you drink from the river
of silence shall you indeed sing.
And when you have reached the mountain top,
then you shall begin to climb.
And when the earth shall claim your limbs,
then you shall truly dance.

~*Kahil Gibran*

For Katrina's Sun-Dial

Time is
Too Slow for those who Wait,
Too Swift for those who Fear,
Too Long for those who Grieve,
Too Short for those who Rejoice;
But for those who Love,
Time is not.

~*Henry Van Dyke*

Death Is Nothing At All

Death is nothing at all,
I have only slipped away into the next room,
I am I, and you are you,
Whatever we were to each other, that we are still,
Call me by my old familiar name,
Speak to me in the same easy way which you always did,
Put no difference into your tone;
Wear no forced air of solemnity or sorrow.
Laugh as we always laughed at the little jokes we enjoyed
together.
Play, smile, think of me, pray for me.
Let my name be the household word that it always was.

Let it be spoken without effect, without the shadow of a
ghost on it.
Life means all that it ever meant.
It is the same as it ever was; there is absolutely unbroken
continuity.
Why should I be out of mind because I am out of sight?
I am just waiting for you, for an interval, somewhere very
near, just around the corner.
All is well.

~Henry Scott Holland

When I die

When I die
Give what's left of me away
To children
And old men that wait to die.
And if you need to cry,
Cry for your brother
Walking the street beside you.
And when you need me,
Put your arms
Around anyone
And give them
What you need to give to me.

I want to leave you something,
Something better
Than words
Or sounds.

Look for me
In the people I've known

Or loved,
And if you cannot give me away,
At least let me live on your eyes
And not on your mind.

You can love me most
By letting
Hands touch hands,
By letting
Bodies touch bodies,
And by letting go
Of children
That need to be free.

Love doesn't die,
People do.
So, when all that's left of me
Is love,
Give me away.

~Author Unknown

    In quitting this strange world, (he/she) has now gone a little ahead of me. This is of little significance. For us believing physicists, the separation of past, present, and future has only the character of an illusion.

~Albert Einstein

Love Will Never Go Away

Spring, and the land lies green
Beneath a yellow sun.
We walked the land together, you and I
And never knew what future days would bring.
Will you often think of me,

When flowers burst forth each year?
When the earth begins to grow again?
Some say death is so final,
But my love for you can never die.
Just as the sun once warmed our hearts,
Let this love touch you some night,
When I am gone,
And the loneliness comes -
Before the dawn begins to scatter
Your dreams away.

Summer, and I never knew a bird
Could sing so sweet and clear,
Until they told me I must leave you
For a while.
I never knew the sky could be so deep a blue,
Until I knew I could not grow old with you
But better to be loved by you,
Than to have lived a million summers,
And never known your love.
Together, let us, you and I
Remember the days and nights,
for eternity.

Fall, and the earth begins to die,
And leaves turn golden-brown upon the trees.
Remember me, too, in autumn, for I will walk with you,
As of old, along a city sidewalk at evening-time,
Though I cannot hold you by the hand.

Winter, and perhaps someday there may be
Another fireplace, another room,
With crackling fire and fragrant smoke,
And turning, suddenly, we will be together,

And I will hear your laughter and touch your face,
And hold you close to me again.
But, until then, if loneliness should seek you out,
Some winter night, when snow is falling down,
Remember, though death has come for me,
Love will never go away.

~Orville Kelly

By Herself and Her Friends

If I should go before the rest of you
Break not a flower nor inscribe a stone,
Nor when I'm gone speak in a Sunday voice
But be the usual selves that I have known.
Weep if you must, Parting is hell,
But Life goes on, So sing as well.

~Joyce Grenfell

Success

He has achieved success
who has lived well,
laughed often, and loved much;

who has enjoyed the trust of
pure women,
the respect of intelligent men and
the love of little children;

who has filled his niche and accomplished his task;
who has left the world better than he found it

whether by an improved poppy,
a perfect poem or a rescued soul;

who has never lacked appreciation of Earth's beauty
or failed to express it;

who has always looked for the best in others and
given them the best he had;

whose life was an inspiration;
whose memory a benediction.

~Bessie-Anderson-Stanley

Crossing Over

Oh, please don't feel guilty
It was just my time to go.
I see you are still feeling sad,
And the tears just seem to flow.
We all come to earth for our lifetime,
And for some it's not many years
I don't want you to keep crying
You are shedding so many tears.
I haven't really left you
Even though it may seem so.
I have just gone to my heavenly home,
And I'm closer to you than you know.
Just believe that when you say my name,
I'm standing next to you,
I know you long to see me,
But there's nothing I can do.
But I'll still send you messages
And hope you understand,

That when your time comes to cross over,
I'll be there to take your hand.

~Author Unknown

Four Candles – Ceremony

The first candle represents our grief.
The pain of losing you is intense.
It reminds us of the depth of our love for you.

This second candle represents our courage.
To confront our sorrow,
To comfort each other,
To change our lives.

This third candle we light in your memory.
For the times we laughed,
The times we cried,
The times we were angry with each other,
The silly things you did,
The caring and joy you gave us.

This fourth candle we light for our love.
We light this candle that your light will always shine.
As we enter this holiday season and share this night of
remembrance with our family and friends.
We cherish the special place in our hearts
that will always be reserved for you.
We thank you for the gift
your living brought to each of us.
We love you.
We remember you.

~Author Unknown

Let Me Go

When I come to the end of the road
And the sun has set for me
I want no rites in a gloom filled room
Why cry for a soul set free?
Miss me a little, but not for long
And not with your head bowed low
Remember the love that once we shared
Miss me, but let me go.

For this is a journey we all must take
And each must go alone.
It's all part of the master plan
A step on the road to home.
When you are lonely and sick at heart
Go to the friends we know.
Laugh at all the things we used to do
Miss me, but let me go.

~Author Unknown

When I Am Gone

When I am gone, release me - let me go
I have so many things to see and do.
You must not tie yourself to me with tears
Be happy that we had so many years.

I gave you love, you can only guess,
how much you gave me in happiness.
I thank you for the love each have shown,
but now it is time I traveled alone.

So grieve awhile for me if grieve you must,
then let your grief be comforted by trust
It is only for a while that we must part
so bless those memories within your heart.
I will not be far away, for life goes on.
so if you need me, call and I will come.

Though you cannot see or touch me, I will be near
And if you listen with your heart, you will hear
All of my love around you, soft and clear.
Then when you must come this way alone,
I will greet you with a smile and a "Welcome Home"

~Anonymous

Do Not Stand at My Grave and Weep

Do not stand at my grave and weep,
I am not there, I do not sleep.
I am a thousand winds that blow,
I am the diamond glints on snow.
I am the sunlight on ripened grain.
I am the gentle autumn rain.
When you awaken in the morning's hush
I am the swift uplifting rush
Of quiet birds in circled flight.
I am the soft stars that shine at night.
Do not stand at my grave and cry;
I am not there, I did not die.

~Mary Elizabeth Frye

Memories Build a Special Bridge

Our memories build a special bridge
when loved ones have to part
to help us feel we're with them still
and sooth a grieving heart.
Our memories span the years we shared,
preserving ties that bind,
They build a special bridge of love
and bring us peace of mind.

~Emily Matthews

Love Lives On

Those we love are never really lost to us
we feel them in so many special ways,
through friends they always cared about
and dreams they left behind,
in beauty that they added to our days ...
in words of wisdom we still carry with us
and memories that never will be gone ...
Those we love are never really lost to us,
For everywhere their special love lives on.

~A. Bradley

While Waiting for Thee

Don't weep at my grave,
For I am not there,
I've a date with a butterfly
To dance in the air.
I'll be singing in the sunshine,
Wild and free,

Playing tag with the wind,
While I'm waiting for thee.

~*Author Unknown*

The Comfort and Sweetness of Peace

After the clouds, the sunshine,
after the winter, the spring,
after the shower, the rainbow,
for life is a changeable thing.
After the night, the morning,
bidding all darkness cease,
after life's cares and sorrows,
the comfort and sweetness of peace.

~*Helen Steiner Rice*

Faith

You will not see me, so you must have faith.
I wait for the time when
we can soar together again, both aware of each other.
Until then, live your life to its fullest
and when you need me, just whisper my name in your heart,
I will be there.

~*Emily Dickenson*

My Little Angel

You've just walked on ahead of me
And I've got to understand
You must release the ones you love
And let go of their hand.
I try and cope the best I can

But I'm missing you so much
If I could only see you
And once more feel your touch.
Yes, you've just walked on ahead of me
Don't worry I'll be fine
But now and then I swear I feel
Your hand slip into mine.

–Author Unknown

Something Beautiful Remains

The tide recedes but leaves behind
bright seashells on the sand.
The sun goes down, but gentle
warmth still lingers on the land.
The music stops, and yet it echoes
on in sweet refrains …
For every joy that passes,
something beautiful remains.

–Author Unknown

Remember Me

To the living, I am gone
To the sorrowful, I will never return
To the angry, I was cheated
But to the happy, I am at peace
And to the faithful, I have never left
I cannot speak, but I can listen
I cannot be seen, but I can be heard
So as you stand upon the shore

70

Gazing at the beautiful sea, remember me
As you look in awe at a mighty forest
And in its grand majesty, remember me
Remember me in your hearts,
In your thoughts, and the memories of the
Times we loved, the times we cried,
the battle we fought and the times we laughed
For if you always think of me,
I will never have gone.

~Anonymous

Humor

Life should not be a journey to the grave with the intention of arriving safely in an attractive and well preserved body, but rather to skid in sideways, chocolate in one hand, martini in the other, body thoroughly used up, totally worn out and screaming 'Woo hoo, what a ride!'

~Author Unknown

The Dragonfly

Once, in a pond, under the lily pads, there lived a water beetle in a community of water beetles. They lived a simple life with few disturbances. Once in a while, sadness would come to the community when one of their fellow beetles would climb the stem of the lily pad and would not be seen again. They knew when this happened; their friend was gone forever. Then, one day, one little beetle felt an irresistible urge to climb up that stem. However, he was determined he would not leave forever. He would come back and tell his friends what he found at the top.

When he reached the top and climbed out of the water onto the surface of the lily pad, he was so tired, and the sun was so warm, he decided he must take a nap.

As he slept, his body changed and when he woke up, he had turned into a beautiful blue-tailed dragonfly with broad wings and a slender body designed for flying. So, fly he did! And, as he soared he saw the beauty of a whole new world and a far superior way of life to what he had ever known existed. Then he remembered his beetle friends and how they thought he was gone forever. He wanted to go back to tell them that he was now more alive than he had been before he left. His life had not ended, but changed. But, his new body would not go down into the water. He could not get back to tell his friends the good news. Then he understood that their time would come, when they too would know what he now knew. So, he raised his wings and flew off into his joyous new life.

~Author Unknown

When I think of death, and of late the idea has come with alarming frequency, I seem at peace with the idea that a day will dawn when I will no longer be among those living in this valley of strange humors.

I can accept the idea of my own demise, but I am unable to accept the death of anyone else. I find it impossible to let a friend or relative go into that country of no return. Disbelief becomes my close companion, and anger often follows in its wake. I answer the heroic question 'Death, where is thy sting?' with 'It is here in my heart and mind and memories.'

~Maya Angelou

We are like children privileged to spend a day in a great park, a park filled with many gardens and playgrounds and azure-tinted lakes with white boats sailing upon the tranquil waves. True, the day allotted to each one of us is not the same in length, in light, in beauty. Some children of earth are privileged to spend a long and sunlit day in the garden of the earth. For others the day is shorter, cloudier, and dusk descends more quickly as in a winter's tale. But whether our life is a long summery day or a shorter wintry afternoon, we know that inevitably there are storms and squalls which overcast even the blues of heaven and there are sunlit rays which pierce the darkest autumn sky. The day that we are privileged to spend in the great park of life is not the same for all human beings, but there is enough beauty and joy and gaiety in the hours if we will but treasure them.

Then for each one of us the moment comes when the great nurse, death, takes man, the child, by the hand and quietly says, 'It is time to go home. Night is coming. It is your bedtime, child of earth. Come, you're tired. Lie down at last in the quiet of the nursery and sleep. Sleep well. The day is gone. Stars shine in the canopy of eternity.

-Joshia L. Liebman, from Peace of Mind

There is sacredness in tears. They are not the mark of weakness, but of power. They speak more eloquently than ten thousand tongues. They are messengers of overwhelming grief, of deep contrition and of unspeakable love.

- Washington Irving

73

Spiritual Readings

Do Not Weep For Me

Do not weep for me, for I have lived …
I have joined my hand with my fellows' hands,
to leave the planet better than I found it.
Do not weep for me, for I have loved and been loved by
my family, by those I loved who loved me back
for I never knew a stranger, only friends.
Do not weep for me.
When you feel the ocean spray upon your face,
I am there.
When your heart beats faster at the dolphin's leaping grace,
I am there.
When you reach out to touch another's heart,
as now I touch God's face,
I am there.
Do not weep for me. I am not gone.

~*Author Unknown* (read for Michael Landon)

Gone from my Sight

I stand upon the seashore. A ship at my side spreads her white sails to the morning breeze and moves softly out to the blue ocean. She is an object of beauty and strength.

I stand and look at her until at length she hangs like a speck of white cloud just where the sea and sky come down to mingle with one another. Then someone at my side exclaims—"Look, she's gone!"

Gone where? Gone from my sight, that's all. She is just as large in mast and hull as she ever was. Her diminished size lies in me, not her. And at the very moment when someone at my side exclaims, "Look, she's gone," there are other eyes eagerly watching her approach, and other voices ready to take up the glad shout, "Look, she's coming!" And that is death.

~Henry Van Dyke

I imagine a person's life is like a beautifully decorated balloon, tethered by a cord to the earth. It is buffeted by every breeze and strains at the restraint with sometimes-harsh movements. Suddenly, a moment comes when the cord is released and the balloon lifts! No longer fighting the wind: it is lifted high upon it, graceful and dancing with heavenly movements. From an earthly point of view it becomes smaller and smaller until it fades from sight. I feel my loss until I remember that the balloon itself is not becoming smaller as it lifts, but larger and larger until at some point it bursts the last vestige of its earthly life and merges with the highest atmosphere. The essence of that balloon, what made it a balloon, becomes totally free and part of the air that touches my face, the power that moves the clouds, even my very breath. In the same way, a soul, merges with the Omnipresent Creator of Life, and is part of the Goodness of God. So they will always be, in some part, present with each of us, as God is present with us now.

~Rev. Maureen Christopher

Clown's Prayer

As I stumble through this life,
help me to create more laughter than tears,
dispense more cheer than gloom,
spread more cheer than despair.

Never let me become so indifferent,
that I will fail to see the wonders in the eyes of a child,
or the twinkle in the eyes of the aged.

Never let me forget that my total effort is to cheer people,
make them happy, and forget momentarily,
all the unpleasantness in their lives.

And in my final moment,
may I hear You whisper:
"When you made my people smile,
you made me smile."

~Author Unknown

I'm Still Here

Friend, please don't mourn for me
I'm still here, though you don't see.
I'm right by your side each night and day
And within your heart I long to stay.

My body is gone but I'm always near.
I'm everything you feel, see or hear.
My spirit is free, but I'll never depart
As long as you keep me alive in your heart.

I'll never wander out of your sight,
I'm the brightest star on a summer night.
I'll never be beyond your reach;
I'm the warm moist sand when you're at the beach.

I'm the colorful leaves when Autumn's around
And the pure white snow that blankets the ground.
I'm the beautiful flowers of which you're so fond,
The clear cool water in a quiet pond.

I'm the first bright blossom you'll see in the spring,
The first warm raindrop that April will bring.
I'm the first ray of light when the sun starts to shine,
And you'll see that the face in the moon is mine.

When you start thinking there's no one to love you,
You can talk to me through the Lord above you.
I'll whisper my answer through the leaves on the trees,
And you'll feel my presence in the soft summer breeze.

I'm the hot salty tears that flow when you weep
And the beautiful dreams that come while you sleep.
I'm the smile you see on a baby's face.
Just look for me, friend, I'm every place!

~Author Unknown

To My Dearest Family

Some things I'd like to say,
but first of all to let you know,
that I arrived okay.
I'm writing this from Heaven
where I dwell with God above,

where there's no more tears or sadness,
there is just eternal love.
Please do not be unhappy
just because I'm out of sight,
remember that I'm with you
every morning, noon and night.
That day I had to leave you
when my life on Earth was through,
God picked me up and hugged me
and He said I welcome you.
It's good to have you back again
you were missed while you were gone,
as for your dearest family
they'll be here later on.
I need you here so badly
as part of My big plan,
there's so much that we have to do
to help our mortal man.
Then God gave me a list of things
He wished for me to do,
and foremost on that list of mine
is to watch and care for you.
And I will be beside you
every day and week and year,
and when you're sad
I'm standing there
to wipe away the tear.
And when you lie in bed at night
the days chores put to flight,
God and I are closest to you
in the middle of the night.
When you think of my life on Earth
and all those loving years,

because you're only human
they are bound to bring you tears.

But do not be afraid to cry
it does relieve the pain,
remember there would be no flowers
unless there was some rain.

I wish that I could tell you
of all that God has planned,
but if I were to tell you
you wouldn't understand.

But one thing is for certain
though my life on Earth is o're,
I am closer to you now
than I ever was before.

And to my very many friends
trust God knows what is best,
I'm still not far away from you
I'm just beyond the crest.

There are rocky roads ahead of you
and many hills to climb,
but together we can do it
taking one day at a time.

It was always my philosophy
and I'd like it for you too,
that as you give unto the World
so the World will give to you.

If you can help somebody
who is in sorrow or in pain,

then you can say to God at night
my day was not in vain.
And now I am contented
that my life it was worthwhile,
knowing as I passed along the way
I made somebody smile.

So if you meet somebody
who is down and feeling low,
just lend a hand to pick him up
as on your way you go.

When you are walking
down the street
and you've got me on your mind,
I'm walking in your footsteps
only half a step behind.

And when you feel the gentle breeze
or the wind upon your face,
that's me giving you a great big hug
or just a soft embrace.

And when it's time for you to go
from that body to be free,
remember you're not going
you are coming here to me.

And I will always love you
from that land way up above,
Will be in touch again soon
P.S. God sends His Love.

–Author Unknown

Song of the River

The snow melts on the mountain
And the water runs down to the spring,
And the spring in a turbulent fountain,
With a song of youth to sing,
Runs down to the riotous river,
And the river flows on to the sea,
And the water again
Goes back in rain
To the hills where it used to be.

And I wonder if Life's deep mystery
Isn't much like the rain and the snow
Returning through all eternity
To the places it used to know.
For life was born on the lofty heights
And flows in a laughing stream
To the river below
Whose onward flow
Ends in a peaceful dream.

And so at last,
When our life has passed
And the river has run its course,
It again goes back,
O'er the selfsame track,
To the mountain which was its source.

So why prize life
Or why fear death,
Or dread what is to be?
The river ran its allotted span
Till it reached the silent sea.

Then the water harked back to the mountaintop
To begin its course once more.
So we shall run the course begun
Till we reach the silent shore,

Then revisit earth in a pure rebirth
From the heart of the virgin snow.
So don't ask why we live or die,
Or wither, or when we go,
Or wonder about the mysteries
That only God may know.

– William Randolph Hearst

I Only Wanted You

They say memories are golden,
well, maybe this is true.
I never wanted memories,
I only wanted you.

A million times I needed you,
a million times I cried.
If love alone could have saved you,
you never would have died.

In life I loved you dearly,
In death I love you still.
Inside my heart you hold a place,
no one could ever fill.

If tears could build a stairway
and heartache make a lane,

I'd walk the path to heaven,
and bring you home again.

Our family chain is broken,
and nothing seems the same.
But as God calls us one by one,
the chain will link again.

~Vicky Holder

The Broken Chain

I little knew that morning. God was going to call your
name,
In life I loved you dearly, in death I do the same.
It broke my heart to loose you, you did not go alone,
for part of me went with you, the day God called you home.
You left me beautiful memories your love is still my guide,
and though we cannot see you, you're always at my side.
Our family chain is broken and nothing seems the same,
but as God calls us one by one, the chain will link again.

~Ron Tranmer

God's Garden

God looked around his garden
And found an empty place,
He then looked down upon the earth
And saw your tired face.
He put his arms around you
And lifted you to rest.
God's garden must be beautiful
He always takes the best.

He knew that you were suffering
He knew you were in pain.
He knew that you would never
Get well on earth again.
He saw the road was getting rough
And the hills were hard to climb.
So he closed your weary eyelids
And whispered, "Peace be thine."
It broke our hearts to lose you
But you didn't go alone,
For part of us went with you
The day God called you home.

-Anonymous

The Day God Took You Home

In tears we saw you sinking,
And watched you pass away.
Our hearts were almost broken,
We wanted you to stay.
But when we saw you sleeping,
So peaceful, free from pain,
How could we wish you back with us,
To suffer that again.
It broke our hearts to lose you,
But you did not go alone,
For part of us went with you,
The day God took you home.

-Anonymous

Poem of Life

Life is but a stopping place,
A pause in what's to be,
A resting place along the road,
to sweet eternity.
We all have different journeys,
Different paths along the way,
We all were meant to learn some things,
but never meant to stay ...
Our destination is a place,
Far greater than we know.
For some the journey's quicker,
For some the journey's slow.
And when the journey finally ends,
We'll claim a great reward,
And find an everlasting peace,
Together with the lord

~Author Unknown

Footprints

One night I dreamed I was walking
Along the beach with the Lord,
Many scenes from my life flashed across the sky.
In each scene I noticed footprints in the sand.
Sometimes there were two sets of footprints.
Other times there was only one.
This bothered me because I noticed
During the low periods of my life when I was
Suffering from anguish, sorrow or defeat,
I could see only one set of footprints.
So I said to the Lord, You promised me,
Lord, that if I followed you,

You would walk with me always.
But I noticed during the most trying periods
Of my life there has only been
One set of prints in the sand.
Why, when I needed you most,
Have you not been there for me?
The Lord replied,
The times when you have seen only one set of footprints
It was then that I carried you.

God Took Him To His Loving Home

God saw him getting tired, a cure was not to be.
He wrapped him in his loving arms
and whispered "Come with me."
He suffered much in silence, his spirit did not bend.
He faced his pain with courage, until the very end.
He tried so hard to stay with us
but his fight was not in vain,
God took him to His loving home
and freed him from the pain.

–Anonymous

A Season

To everything there is a season,
and a time to every purpose under the heaven:
A time to be born, and a time to die;
a time to plant, and a time to pluck up that which is planted;
A time to weep, and a time to laugh;
a time to mourn, and a time to dance;
A time to get, and a time to lose;

a time to keep, and a time to cast away;
A time to rend, and a time to sew;
a time to keep silence, and a time to speak;
A time to love, and a time to hate;
a time of war, and a time of peace.

Before the sublime mystery of life and spirit, the mystery of infinite space and endless time, we stand in reverent awe. This much we know: we are at least one phase of the immortality of life. The mighty stream of life flows on, and, in this mighty stream, we too flow on ... not lost ... but each eternally significant. For this I feel: The spirit never betrays the person who trusts it. Physical life may be defeated but life goes on; character survives, goodness lives and love is immortal.

~Col Robert G. Ingersoll

The Lord's Prayer (Matthew 6:9)

Our Father, who art in heaven, hallowed be thy name.
Thy Kingdom come, thy will be done,
on earth as it is in heaven.
Give us this day our daily bread,
And forgive us our trespasses,
as we forgive those who trespass against us.
And lead us not into temptation,
but deliver us from evil.
For thine is the kingdom, the power and the glory,
forever and ever. Amen

The Lord Is My Shepherd (Psalm 23)

The Lord is my shepherd; I shall not want.
He maketh me to lie down in green pastures:
He leadeth me beside the still waters.
He restoreth my soul: he leadeth me in the paths of right-eousness for his name's sake.
Yea, though I walk through the valley of the shadow of death, I will fear no evil: for thou art with me; thy rod and thy staff they comfort me.
Thou preparest a table before me in the presence of mine enemies: thou anointest my head with oil; my cup runneth over.
Surely goodness and mercy shall follow me all the days of my life: and I will dwell in the house of the Lord forever.

2 Corinthians 5:1

For we know that if the earthly tent we live in is de-stroyed, we have a building from God, a house not made with hands, eternal in the heavens.

Revelation 21:1-4

Then I saw a new heaven and a new earth; for the first heaven and the first earth had passed away, and the sea was no more. And I saw the holy city, new Jerusalem, coming down out of heaven from God, prepared as a bride adorned for her husband; and I heard a loud voice from the throne saying, "Behold, the dwelling of God is with men. He will dwell with them, and they shall be his people, and God himself will be with them; he will wipe away every tear from their eyes, and death shall be no more, neither shall there be mourning nor crying nor pain any more, for the former things have passed away."

1 Thessalonians 4:13

Brothers and sisters, we do not want you to be uninformed about those who sleep in death, so that you do not grieve like the rest of mankind, who have no hope.

Corinthians 13:7-8

Love bears all things, believes all things, hopes all things, endures all things. Love never ends.

II Corinthians 1:7

God will tenderly comfort you ... He will give you strength to endure.

For Mother - Grandmother

The Magic of a Mother's Touch

There's magic in a Mother's touch,
and sunshine in her smile.
There's love in everything she does
to make our lives worthwhile.
We can find both hope and courage
Just by looking in her eyes.
Her laughter is a source of joy,
her works are warm and wise.
There is a kindness and compassion
to be found in her embrace,
and we see the light of heaven
shining from a Mother's face.

~Anonymous

My Mother Kept A Garden

My Mother kept a garden.
A garden of the heart;
She planted all the good things,
That gave my life it's start.

She turned me to the sunshine,
And encouraged me to dream:
Fostering and nurturing
The seeds of self-esteem.

And when the winds and rains came,
She protected me enough;

But not too much, she knew I'd need
To stand up strong and tough.

Her constant good example,
Always taught me right from wrong;
Markers for my pathway
To last my whole life long.

I am my Mother's garden,
I am her legacy.
And I hope today she feels the love,
Reflected back from me.

—Author Unknown

A Mother's Love

A Mother's love is something
that no one can explain,
It is made of deep devotion
and of sacrifice and pain,
It is endless and unselfish
and enduring come what may
For nothing can destroy it
or take that love away . . .
It is patient and forgiving
when all others are forsaking,
And it never fails or falters
even though the heart is breaking . . .
It believes beyond believing
when the world around condemns,
And it glows with all the beauty
of the rarest, brightest gems . . .

It is far beyond defining,
it defies all explanation,
And it still remains a secret
like the mysteries of creation …
A many splendored miracle
man cannot understand
And another wondrous evidence
of God's tender guiding hand.

-Helen Steiner Rice

Irish Funeral Prayer

You can only have one mother
Patient kind and true;
No other friend in all the world,
Will be the same to you.

When other friends forsake you,
To mother you will return,
For all her loving kindness,
She asks nothing in return.

As we look upon her picture,
Sweet memories we recall,
Of a face so full of sunshine,
And a smile for one and all.

Sweet Jesus, take this message,
To our dear mother up above;
Tell her how we miss her,
And give her all our love.

-Author Unknown

For Father - Grandfather

What Makes A Dad

God took the strength of a mountain,
The majesty of a tree,
The warmth of a summer sun,
The calm of a quiet sea,
The generous soul of nature,
The comforting arm of night,
The wisdom of the ages,
The power of the eagle's flight,
The joy of a morning in spring,
The faith of a mustard seed,
The patience of eternity,
The depth of a family need,
Then God combined these qualities,
When there was nothing more to add,
He knew His masterpiece was complete,
And so, He called it ... "Dad."

~Author Unknown

Our Father Kept A Garden

Our Father kept a garden.
A garden of the heart;
He planted all the good things,
That gave our lives their start.

93

He turned us to the sunshine,
And encouraged us to dream:
Fostering and nurturing
The seeds of self-esteem.

And when the winds and rain came,
He protected us enough;
But not too much because he knew
We would stand up strong and tough.

His constant good example,
Always taught us right from wrong;
Markers for our pathway that will last
a lifetime long.

We are our Fathers garden,
We are his legacy.
Thank you, Dad, we love you.

~Author Unknown

Memories

The love we have for (Dad/Father/Granddad)
Will never fade away.
We'll think of him, our special friend
Throughout each passing day.
We'll walk into the room
And see his empty chair;
Although we know he's resting,
We'll feel his presence there.
The memories of his laughter,
His warm and loving smile,
His eyes so full of happiness,
His heart that of a child.

Memories are forever
Be they laughter or of tears,
Memories we will treasure
Through all the forthcoming years.

~Author Unknown

Quotes

These brief wording selections can be used to convey a sentiment in a variety of ways. A quote can be added to the memorial program, incorporated into the eulogy, shared as a reading in the memorial service, etc.

Butterfly ...
As you danced in the light with joy,
Love lifted you. As you brushed against this world so gently,
You lifted us.

~T.C. Ring

Life is eternal; love is immortal; and death is only a horizon; and a horizon is nothing save the limit of our sight.

~Raymond Rossiter

As a well-spent day brings happy sleep,
so life well used brings happy death.

~Leonardo da Vinci

I know for certain that we never lose the people we love, even to death. They continue to participate in every act, thought and decision we make. Their love leaves an indelible imprint in our memories. We find comfort in knowing that our lives have been enriched by having shared their love.

~Leo Buscaglia

When you come to the edge of all that you have known, there will be two possibilities awaiting you: There will be something solid to stand on or you will be taught how to fly.

~from "After goodbye: an AIDS story"

From joy all beings have come and unto joy they all return.

~Upanishads

If there ever comes a day when we can't be together, keep me in your heart, I'll stay there forever.

~A.A. Milne (from Winnie the Pooh)

The spirit is the life of the body seen from within, and the body the outward manifestation of the life of the spirit—the two being really one.

~Jung

The soul of a man is immortal and imperishable.

~Plato

And in the end, it's not the years in your life that count. It's the life in your years.

~Abraham Lincoln

"Are we going to be friends forever?" asked Piglet.
"Even longer," Pooh answered.

~A.A. Milne (from Winnie the Pooh)

These, then, are my last words to you: Be not afraid of life. Believe that life is worth living, and your belief will help create that fact.

~ William James

If we've been pleased with life, we shouldn't be displeased with death, since it comes from the hand of the same master.

~Michelangelo

When someone we love dies, our relationship with them doesn't end, it changes from a physical one to a spiritual one.

~Author Unknown

Yesterday is a memory, tomorrow is
a mystery and today is a gift,
which is why it is called the present.
What the caterpillar perceives is the end;
to the butterfly is just the beginning.
Everything that has a beginning has an ending.
Make your peace with that and all will be well

~Buddhist Saying

It is not length of life, but depth of life.

~Emerson Ralph Waldo

❖

When you were born, you cried and the world rejoiced. Live your life in a manner so that when you die the world cries and you rejoice.

~Native American Proverb

❖

Death is more universal than life; everyone dies but not everyone lives.

~A. Sachs

❖

Every man dies. Not every man really lives.

~William Wallace

The grave is but a covered bridge, leading from light to light, through a brief darkness.

~Henry Wadsworth Longfellow

❖

I've told my children that when I die, to release balloons in the sky to celebrate that I graduated. For me, death is a graduation.

~Elisabeth Kubler-Ross

❖

Death leaves a heartache no one can heal, love leaves a memory no one can steal.

~Anonymous

❖

To live in hearts we leave behind is not to die.

~Clyde Campbell

❖

If you live to be a hundred, I want to live to be a hundred minus one day, so I never have to live without you.

~A.A. Milne (from Winnie the Pooh)

While we are mourning the loss of our friend, others are rejoicing to meet him behind the veil.

~J Taylor

Death ends a life, not a relationship.

~Jack Lemmon

When words are most empty, tears are most apt.

~Max Lucado

I have passed the mountain peak and my soul is soaring in the firmament of complete and unbounded freedom; I am in comfort, I am in peace.

~Kahlil Gibran

Hope is the thing with feathers that perches in the soul, and sings the tune without the words, and never stops at all.

~Emily Dickenson

Here is a thought from **"The Little Prince"** ...

"In one of the stars I shall be living. In one of them I shall be laughing. And so it will be as if all the stars were laughing, when you look at the sky at night."

~Antoine de Saint-Exupéry

So when you look up at the night sky, and see the twinkle of the stars, imagine, (*name*), smiling back at you.

A death is not the extinguishing of a light, but the putting out of the lamp because the dawn has come.

~Author Unknown

Seashells remind us that every passing life leaves something beautiful behind.

~Author Unknown

How very softly you tiptoed into our world, almost silently, only a moment you stayed. But what an imprint your footsteps have left upon our hearts.

~Dorothy Ferguson

(For a child)
They say that time in heaven is compared to "the blink of an eye" for us on this earth. Sometimes it helps me to think of my child running ahead of me through a beautiful field of wildflowers and butterflies; so happy and

completely caught up in what she is doing that when she looks behind her, I'll already be there.

~Author Unknown

Loss of life is to be mourned, but only if the life was wasted.

~ Mr. Spock (Star Trek)

     Death changes us, the living. In the presence of death, we become more aware of life ... It can inspire us to decide what really matters in life—and then to seek it.

~Candy Lightner

Readings for Pets

You came into my life one day
So beautiful and smart,
My dear and sweet companion,
I loved you from the start.
Although we knew the time would come
When we would have to part,
You'll never be forgotten,
You left paw prints on my heart.

~Author Unknown

Words of Wisdom From Our Furry Canine Friends

When loved ones come home, always run to greet them.
Never pass up the opportunity to go for a joyride.
Allow the experience of fresh air and the wind in your face to be pure ecstasy.
When it's in your best interest, practice obedience.
Let others know when they've invaded your territory.
Take naps.
Stretch before rising.
Run, romp, and play daily.
Thrive on attention and let people touch you.
Avoid biting when a simple growl will do.
On warm days, stop to lie on your back in the grass.
On hot days, drink lots of water and lie under a shady tree.
When you're happy, dance around and wag your entire body.
No matter how often you're scolded, don't buy into the guilt thing and pout.
Run right back and make friends.
Delight in the simple joy of a long walk.
Eat with gusto and enthusiasm.
Stop when you have had enough.
Be loyal.
Never pretend to be something you're not.
If what you want lies buried, dig until you find it.
When someone is having a bad day, be silent, sit close by and nuzzle them gently.

~Author Unknown

Heavenly Father, Creator of all things, thank you for having entrusted us with (*name*).

Thank you for letting (him/her) teach us unselfish love.
Thank you for the memories that we can recall to brighten
our days for the rest of our lives.
Finally, in gratitude, we return (*name*) to you.
Amen.

~Author Unknown

My friend

When God made the earth and the sky
The flowers and the trees
He made all the animals
All the birds and the bees.

And when His work was finished
No one was quite the same.
He said, "I'll walk this earth of mine
And give each one a name."

So He traveled land and sea
And everywhere He went
A little creature followed Him
Until its strength was spent.
When all were named upon the earth
And in the sky and sea
A little creature said, "Dear Lord
There's not one left for me."

The Father smiled and softly said
I've left you to the end
I've turned my own name back to front and called you
'Dog' my friend."

~Harold Wilson

104

A Brilliant Rainbow

High on whispered wings I fly,
a radiant star, I light the sky.
Toward the sun I soar so free,
a brilliant rainbow follows me.
I pulsate through your very soul
and in my paws your heart I hold.
The day will come when you'll fly too,
I'll be there to welcome you.
Until the time we meet again,
I won't journey far my friend.
For in your love I live so free,
a brilliant rainbow guiding me.

~Terri Onorato

You'll Meet Me in the Light

I know that you can't see me,
but trust me I'm right here.
Although I'm up in heaven,
my love for you stays near.
So often I see you crying,
many times you call my name.
I want so much to lick your face
and ease some of your pain.
I wish that I could make you see
that Heaven indeed is real.
If you could see me run and play
how much better you would feel.

But our loving God has promised me
that when the time is right,
you'll step out of the darkness and
meet me in the light.

~Author Unknown

Understanding Grief

"When a person plays a role of such mass and significance in one's life, one assumes that the whole of creation feels the moment of his exit too, that the severing is as severe and deeply felt."

~David Crowder

While there is no one correct way to respond or to support someone who is grieving, here are some general guidelines that may help to offer comfort, as well as prevent saying or doing something that unintentionally causes the grief-stricken person additional pain.

Grief is a personal experience.

We may believe we would do things differently if it had happened to us. Or we may think we're helping by telling someone what they should feel or be focused on, i.e. "You should feel relieved, they are no longer in pain."

Although we may think we're helping them by focusing on the positive, what we're really saying is, "You shouldn't feel what you're feeling, you should feel something else."

This excerpt from the book, "My Bright Abyss," beautifully illustrates the experience of loss:

From the moment I learned of _____'s death, not only was the world not intensified, it was palpably attenuated. I can still feel how far away everything—the people walking on the street beyond the window, the books on the shelf, my wife smiling up at me in the moment before I told her—suddenly seemed. And long after the initial shock, I felt a maddening, muffled quality to the world around me—which, paradoxically, went hand in hand with the most acute, interior sensations of pain. It seemed as if the numbness was not mine, but the world's, as if some energy had drained out of things. At some point I realized that for all my literary talk of the piquancy and poignancy that mortality imparts to immediate experience, part of my enjoyment of life had always been an unconscious assumption of its continuity. Life is short, we say, in one way or another, but in truth, because we cannot imagine our own death until it is thrust upon us, we live in a land where only other people die.

-adapted from "My Bright Abyss," by **Christian Wiman**

Their loss cannot be fixed. We cannot make their pain go away. So, allow them to feel whatever they're feeling without trying to make them feel differently. Be willing to sit quietly with them and their pain.

Remind them not to fight their grief or try to control it. Encourage them to simply move along with it and let it take them wherever it goes, experience their feelings and share the painful memories. They don't need others to give them permission to grieve, they can give that permission to themselves.

The following are some common phrases that well-intentioned people say when someone dies, which cause pain and should be avoided:

When an infant dies, "At least you didn't get attached," or "You can have other babies."
At least she/he didn't suffer.
At least you had time to say goodbye.
I know how you feel.
Only the good die young.
You're strong. You can handle it.
God wanted more flowers for His garden.
Keep a stiff upper lip.
It's a blessing.
You'll be fine.
Time heals all wounds.

Be specific when you offer help.

We can lessen their burden during this time by offering to take care of some of their day-to-day tasks. Instead of saying, "Let me know if you need anything," make a specific offer: "May I come by tomorrow around 5 p.m. and bring you dinner?"

If we offer help that requires them to ask for something, it is unlikely that they will. Not because they don't have a need, but because identifying a need, figuring out whom to call, and then calling to ask, is far beyond their capacity at this time.

The Stages of Grief

In 1969, the psychiatrist, Elisabeth Kübler-Ross, identified 5 distinct phases of grief that people experience as a result of loss. While knowing about these phases may help us to appreciate and be patient with the process, even Dr. Kubler-Ross believed, "They were never meant to help tuck messy emotions into neat packages. They are responses to loss that many people have, but there is not a typical response to loss, as there is no typical loss. Our grieving is as individual as our lives."

This list is meant to provide comfort to someone who is grieving, to reassure that his or her feelings are not unusual.

- **Denial:** "This can't be happening to me."
- **Anger:** "*Why* is this happening? Who is to blame?"
- **Bargaining:** "Make this not happen, and in return I will …"
- **Depression:** "I'm too sad to do anything."
- **Acceptance:** "I'm at peace with what happened."

Experiencing these emotions at various times following a loss is natural. However, overanalyzing the process can lead to avoidance of the natural grief process. A belief that sadness over a loss has a time limit, can lead to depression. "The truth is that grief is as unique as a fingerprint, conforms to no timetable or societal expectation," says, Patrick O'Malley in his article, "Getting Grief Right."

Dr. O'Malley believes that the story of loss has three chapters. "Chapter 1 has to do with attachment: the strength of the bond with the person who has been lost. Understanding the relationship between degree of attachment and intensity of grief brings great relief for most patients." He often tells his patients that the size of their grief corresponds to the depth of their love.

"Chapter 2" he says, "is the death event itself. This is often the moment when the person experiencing the loss begins to question his sanity, particularly when the death is premature and traumatic." One of his patients had prided herself on her ability to stay in control in difficult times. "The profound emotional chaos of her baby's death made her feel crazy. As soon as she was able, she resisted the craziness and shut down the natural pain and suffering."

"Chapter 3," he says, "is the long road that begins after the last casserole dish is picked up—when the outside world stops grieving with you." His patient "wanted to reassure her family, friends and herself that she was on the fast track to closure. This was exhausting. What she really needed was to let herself sink into her sadness, accept it."

Mourning

We all grieve when someone we love dies, but healing happens when we mourn. Grief is what you think and feel on the inside, mourning is the outward expression of those thoughts and feelings. To mourn is to be an active participant in the grief journey and the next step to wholeness.

Mourning is when you take the grief you have on the inside and express it outside of yourself. Another way of looking at it is "grief gone public" or "the outward expression of grief." Mourning integrates the death into our ongoing lives, by openly and honestly expressing the thoughts and feelings from the inside to the outside—no pretense, no repression, and no inhibitions.

After the Service
Following Up

Once the service is over and a few weeks have gone by, it's time to think about reaching out to the family. In the weeks following the memorial, most who attended the service have gone back to their regular lives—life has moved on ... for them. But the family will still be immersed in the various stages of grief. It can be a comfort to them to know that someone is still thinking about them and the loss of their loved one.

Approximately 2 weeks after the memorial, you could send a brief note, letting them know you are thinking of them. Then, on the next birthday of the deceased, you could send a card to the family, acknowledging this special day. If they were married, you could send a card to their widow at the first anniversary following the death of their loved one.

If you would like to reach out to the family through-out the first year, you could send a note, once a quarter, acknowledging what they may be experiencing at that time and reassuring them that their grief is normal and helpful for healing. There is also a set of four books that you can purchase through, Stephens Ministries titled, "Journeying Through Grief." One book is sent each quarter and focuses on what the person is likely experiencing at that point in grief—offering understanding, empathy, compassion and hope. These books do reference God, but are not overly religious.

Here are some sample follow-up notes:

Note #1
Timing: Send approximately 3 weeks after the memorial)

I've been thinking of you these past several weeks and I want to express my continuing sorrow for your loss.

I also want to let you know that you don't have to fight your grief or try to control it. Simply move along with it and let it take you wherever it goes—experience the feelings and share the painful memories. You don't need permission from others to grieve—give that permission to yourself.

May you allow yourself to feel what you feel and begin the process of healing.

Sincerely,
<your name>

Note #2
Timing: Send approximately 3 months after the memorial

After a few months have passed, it can seem as if the rest of the world has gone back to life as usual—while you may be wondering what "life as usual" even means. Again, remember to give yourself permission to grieve in whatever way you need to, for as long as you need. Grief is as individual as we are.

May you continue to allow yourself to grieve in your own unique way.

Sincerely,
<*your name*>

Note #3
Timing: Send approximately 6 months after the memorial

It is perfectly all right and completely normal for you to still be grieving 6 months after a loss. This is good for you to know because, if your experience is anything like that of many others who have lost a loved one, you may be feeling a lot of pressure to "get over it" and "move on" with your life. To the rest of the world, half a year is plenty of time to "heal." But when you've lost someone you love, six months can seem like no time at all. Don't let yourself be pressured or rushed—take all the time you need to grieve.

May you continue to take all the time you need to allow yourself to grieve in your own unique way.

Sincerely,
<*your name*>

Note #4
Timing: Send approximately 11 months after the memorial

I know it will soon be 1 year since ＿＿＿ died. The first anniversary of the loss of a loved one can be a difficult day. People often begin to feel anxious weeks beforehand.

Give yourself renewed permission to grieve. This is important because you may have people around you asserting that your grief should have ended a long time ago. But you can't grieve by someone else's timetable. Let yourself grieve for as long as you need to grieve.

May you continue to be gentle with yourself and take all the time you need to heal.

Sincerely,
<your name>

Disposition of the Body

Disposition refers to the way in which human remains are handled. The most common methods of disposition are burial or cremation. With either of these options, there are a variety of ways to have the deceased's remains present at the service.

Burial

Prior to burial, providing a viewing of the deceased's body can be a comfort and offer closure to the grieving, but some may not want to view the body or this option may not be possible. The viewing can be private and offered in a separate room from the service, or open casket in the same room as the funeral for loved ones to view at a designated time during or after the service.

Cremation

If the deceased is to be cremated, the urn containing the ashes could be placed on the altar during the service.

Another option for cremation is to scatter the ashes in a location that was meaningful to the deceased, such as, the side of a mountain where they enjoyed hiking, a lake where they frequently fished, etc. Some people leave specific instructions for where they want their ashes scattered. Laws concerning scattering ashes will need to be consulted and differ in each state.

There is also a Seattle-based company, "Artful Ashes," which "memorializes your loved one's ashes in beautiful glass art." Their "artists, capture the essence of your loved ones spirit in a swirl of color and ashes, sealed forever within beautiful glass art."

Whether or not the body is present, it's common to display photos showing highlights of the deceased's life at the service.

How to Write an Obituary

Writing an obituary is a way to honor your loved one's life as well as to announce their death. It can be a painful process, but it's a way to celebrate your loved one's passions, achievements, and surviving family members. A typical obituary has five parts: the announcement of the death, biographical information, survivor information, scheduled services, and contributions.

Here are some basic things to include in the obituary:

- First and last name
- Age
- Birth date, Birthplace
- Residence (city and state)
- Partner's name and other survivor's names
- Education and/or Vocation
- Information or anecdotes that show personality traits

- When and where the funeral, viewing, wake, or memorial service will take place
- Instructions for making donations instead of sending flowers (optional)

If you don't know when the memorial will take place yet, you can include the name of the memorial location so people can contact the venue for more information. If you plan on running the obituary in the newspaper more than once, you can include this information the next time if you know it then.

Obituary Example:

Jane Smith, 71, of Bremerton, died February 12, 2014, with her family by her side. She was born to John and Amy Jones, March 20, 1943, in Nashville, Tennessee. Jane received a BA in Liberal Arts from the University of Tennessee and was a librarian until she retired in 2007. She was passionate about spreading her love for reading throughout her community and in 1995 she was honored with the Bremerton Librarian of the Year award.

Jane is survived by three children: Jan White, Jacob Smith, and Mary Harris. She is also survived by seven grandchildren and three great-grandchildren. Instead of flowers, the family requests that donations be made to the Bremerton Literacy Foundation. A memorial will be held at 3 p.m. Saturday at the Bremerton Funeral Home.

Planning Your Own Eulogy

When writing your own eulogy, you have a unique opportunity to contribute meaningful and especially personal information for your memorial service as well as ensure that your loved ones know how important they were to you.

In addition to the information gathered in the "How to Write a Eulogy" section of this book, here are some ideas to help you enhance your own eulogy.

From Aging with Dignity's *"Five Wishes - Wish #5: My Wish For What I Want My Loved Ones To Know"* here are some thoughts to consider sharing in your own words with your friends and family after you're gone.

- I wish to have my family and friends know that I love them.
- I wish to be forgiven for the times I have hurt my family, friends, and others.

- I wish to have my family, friends and others know that I forgive them for when they may have hurt me in my life.
- I wish for my family and friends to know that I do not fear death itself. I think it is not the end, but a new beginning for me.

One of the significant aspects of leaving a legacy is, how you want people to remember you. What do you consider your most important contribution to this world?

I want to be remembered for ...

To complete the personalization of your memorial service, you may want to include some of your favorite music and/or writings. These selections can be chosen either to evoke fond memories of you, or to characterize some aspect of your personality or beliefs.

I want my memorial service to include the following (music, songs, readings or any other specific requests that you may have) ...

Other wishes: What other wishes do you have that you would like carried out after you're gone? For example, you may wish to designate a charity to receive memorial contributions in lieu of flowers.

Sample Services

Memorial (Non-spiritual) Sample Service

Welcome

You'll notice on the front of your program, below (*name*)'s name, are the dates when (he/she) was born and when (he/she) passed away. (*date*) "dash" (*date*). We all have a date when we entered this world. We will all have a date when we'll leave this world. The "dash" is how we lived our life. We don't get to choose our date of birth, or our date of death, but we do get to choose how we spend the time in-between. (*name*)'s "dash" was filled with love, with life, and with bringing joy to many during (his/her) time on earth.

As a (father/mother), (grandfather/grandmother), (brother/sister), (uncle/aunt) and dear friend to many, (he/she) will be remembered by each of us as someone who touched our lives.

Eulogy (Specific information about the deceased's life)

Address/Reading

Those we love are never really lost to us, we feel them in so many special ways—through friends they always cared about and dreams they left behind, in beauty that they added to our days ... in words of wisdom we still carry with us and memories that never will be gone.

Those we love are never really lost to us—for everywhere their special love lives on.

~A. Bradley

And, (*name*), too is not lost to us. So, let's take this time, to remember (*name*) ... if you have any memories, thoughts or stories you'd like to share, we invite you to do that now.

<Time for people to share their memories>

Closing Words

As we conclude this service, I leave you with these thoughts ...

There is no answer to death but to live and to live vigorously and beautifully. We give respect and dignity to the one we mourn only when we respect and dignify life and when we live life to the fullest. The best of all answers to death is the continuing affirmation of life. Now, for us, the living, may the love of friends, the joy of memories and our hopes for the future give us strength and peace that we may go forward together.

~Gail Mccabe

Memorial (Spiritual) Sample Service

Welcome

Today is a time of remembrance and celebration of (*name*)'s life and all that (he/she) taught us about living.

Eulogy (Specific information about the deceased's life)

Address

The Bible says, "To be absent from the body is to be present with the Lord." From the moment (*name*) breathed (his/her) last breath here on Earth, (he/she) was instantly at home in the presence of God and (his/her) family, surrounded by peace and joy!

It has been said that God never sees His children die; He only sees them come home.

(*name*)'s brother, (*name*), shared this thought shortly after (*name*)'s passing, "I know our father will be waiting for (him/her), in fact, I know what he will say to (him/her); "Hello Little Man."

The Bible, in Philippians 1:3 says … "I thank my God every time I remember you."

And, so, at this time, we will use this opportunity to remember (*name*) … if you have any memories, thoughts or stories you'd like to share, we invite you to do that now.

<Time for people to share their memories>

And now, I will read a poem that his daughter, (*name*) selected.

Ascension
And if I go,
while you're still here ...
Know that I live on,
vibrating to a different measure
behind a thin veil you cannot see through.
You will not see me,
so you must have faith.
I wait for the time when we can soar together again,
both aware of each other.
Until then, live your life to its fullest.
And when you need me,
Just whisper my name in your heart,
... I will be there.

~Colleen Corah Hitchcock

Here is a thought from the book, "The Little Prince" ...

> *"In one of the stars I shall be living. In one of them I shall be laughing. And so it will be as if all the stars were laughing, when you look at the sky at night."*

So when you look up at the night sky, and see the twinkle of the stars, imagine (*name*) smiling back at you.

Closing Prayer
Let us pray ...
Father in heaven,
We thank you because you made us in your own image and gave us gifts in mind, body and spirit. We thank you now for (*name*) and what (he/she) meant to each of us. The gift that (he/she) was to each of our lives. As we honor

(his/her) memory, make us more aware that you are the one from whom comes every perfect gift. Amen.

And now let's close together with the Lord's Prayer ...

Our Father, who art in heaven,
hallowed be thy name;
thy kingdom come; thy will be done
on Earth as it is in heaven.
Give us this day our daily bread;
and forgive us our trespasses
as we forgive those who trespass against us;
and lead us not into temptation,
but deliver us from evil.
For the kingdom, the power,
and the glory are yours
forever and ever.
Amen.

Graveside (Spiritual) Service

Welcome

We gather together today to commit (*name*), to (his/her) final resting place beside (his/her) (husband/wife) and one true love, (*name*). We gather to comfort each other in our grief and to honor the life (*name*) led. A life that was full of hope, happiness, laughter, and love ... through good times as well as in bad. This is the way we'll always remember (*name*) ... that (he/she) lived (his/her) life as an example to each and every person (he/she) met.

Eulogy

(Specific information about the deceased's life)

[Optional: If the graveside service follows a memorial or funeral service, the eulogy at the graveside is not necessary]

Committal

Those who wish to may now come forward and take this soil in your hand and bless (*name*)'s final resting place here beside (his/her) (husband/wife). If any of you have final words for (*name*), please feel free to share them.

Closing Blessing

May we find the courage to face the changes which life presents to us as we go on from here. Give to those who most deeply feel this loss the comfort of your presence, and enable each of us to minister to those who mourn. Amen.

Graveside (Non-spiritual) Service

Welcome

    We gather together today to commit (*name*), to (his/her) final resting place. We have come together from different places, and we're all at different stages on our journey through life. Our paths are varied and we look at life in different ways. But there is one thing we all have in common, at one point or another, and to some degree or other, our lives have been touched by the life of (*name*).

Eulogy

    (Specific information about the deceased's life)

[Optional: If the graveside service follows a memorial or funeral service, the eulogy at the graveside is not necessary]

Committal

    Those who wish to, may now come forward and take a flower and offer a wish for (*name*). If any of you have final words for (*name*), please feel free to share them.

Closing Words

    Let's remind ourselves that (*name*) doesn't live in the grave, but in our hearts and minds.

    Hold on to (*name*) in your thoughts: there is no need to part from (him/her) too hastily. Talk about (him/her) often, repeat the words and sayings (he/she) used, and the jokes (he/she) made, and enjoy your memories of (him/her), just as we have, here today.

About the Author

Dayna Reid, Bestselling Author, Writer, and Minister. She has officiated weddings for over 14 years. Her love for people and the desire to provide couples with a non-judgmental and personalized approach to selecting the words spoken at their wedding inspired her to seek ministry ordination. Although Dayna personally believes in God, she also believes that "everyone has to find their own way in this world, including any beliefs they may have about the mysteries. Because truly, all we really have is a faith in what we believe to be true."

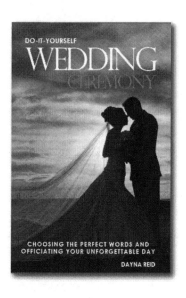